My Little Book of Dump Trucks and Diggers

by Honor Head

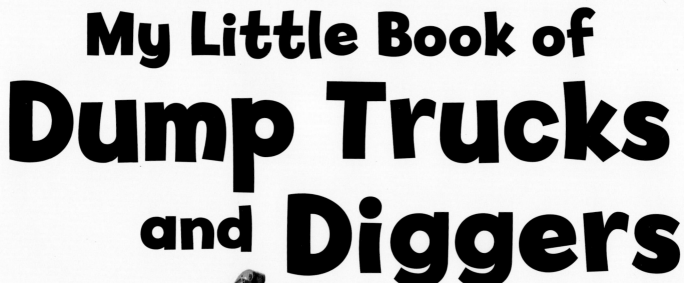

Quarto is the authority on a wide range of topics.

Quarto educates, entertains and enriches the lives of our readers—enthusiasts and lovers of hands-on living.

www.quartoknows.com

Editor: Harriet Stone
Designer: Miranda Snow

This library edition published in 2022 by Quarto Library, an imprint of The Quarto Group.
The Old Brewery, 6 Blundell Street,
London N7 9BH, United Kingdom.
T (0)20 7700 6700 F (0)20 7700 8066
www.QuartoKnows.com

Distributed in the United States and Canada by
Lerner Publishing Services
241 First Avenue North
Minneapolis, MN 55401 U.S.A
www.lernerbooks.com

A CIP record for this book is available from the Library of Congress.

ISBN 978 0 7112 7146 3

Manufactured in Guangdong, China TT072021

MIX
Paper from responsible sources
FSC® C016973
FSC
www.fsc.org

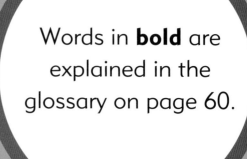

Words in **bold** are explained in the glossary on page 60.

Contents

Big Machines   4

Diggers

What is a Digger?   6
Early Diggers   8
Parts of a Digger   10
Buckets   12
Rippers   14
Loaders   16
Mining Excavators   18
Demolition   20
Grabbers   22
Tunnelers   24
Drill Rigs   26
Bulldozers   28
Compactors   30

Suction Excavators   32
Biggest and Smallest   34

Dump Trucks

What is a Dump Truck?   36
Early Dump Trucks   38
Parts of a Dump Truck   40
Tipping Trucks   42
Concrete Mixers   44
Robot Trucks   46
Snow Plows   48
Combine Harvesters   50
Giant Dump Trucks   52
Road Trains   54
Biggest and Smallest   56
Other Types of Truck   58
Glossary   60
Index   62

Big Machines

Dump **Trucks**, diggers, loaders, and bulldozers are all types of **construction** vehicles. These big machines help to build roads, bridges, tunnels, and tall buildings.

Some construction vehicles carry materials for building. Others have tools for digging, lifting, and pushing.

>> Big machines need very powerful **engines**.

<< A vehicle's big wheels help it to carry heavy **loads** on rough ground.

785B

What is a Digger?

Diggers can pull up trees, scoop up earth, or knock down buildings.

⌄ Tracks stop the digger from sinking into soft mud.

⌃ Crawler tracks work better than wheels on rough ground.

Diggers are used with dump trucks to clear away earth and **rubble** in mines and **quarries**, and on building sites.

⌃ Diggers have buckets with strong teeth for digging.

Early Diggers

Before industrial vehicles, horses were used to pull different machines. The first digger to use steam was the Darby Steam-Digger from 1879.

<< Robert Hasler driving the first Darby Steam-Digger which he helped to build.

>> Modern diggers run on gas and can lift much heavier loads.

Since then, diggers have gradually gotten bigger and much more powerful, helping to build massive structures on construction sites.

Parts of a Digger

A digger has three main parts—a **cab**, an arm, and an **attachment**. The attachment is usually a **bucket** with teeth. The bucket scoops up soil and stones.

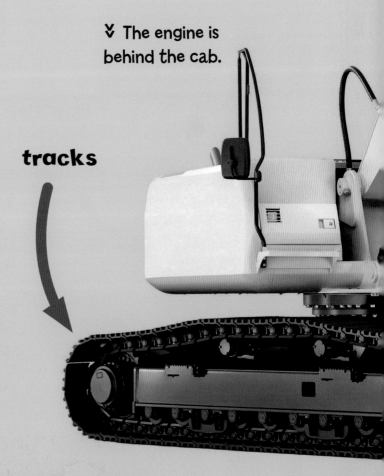

˅ The engine is behind the cab.

tracks

˄ The driver sits in the cab and controls the digger.

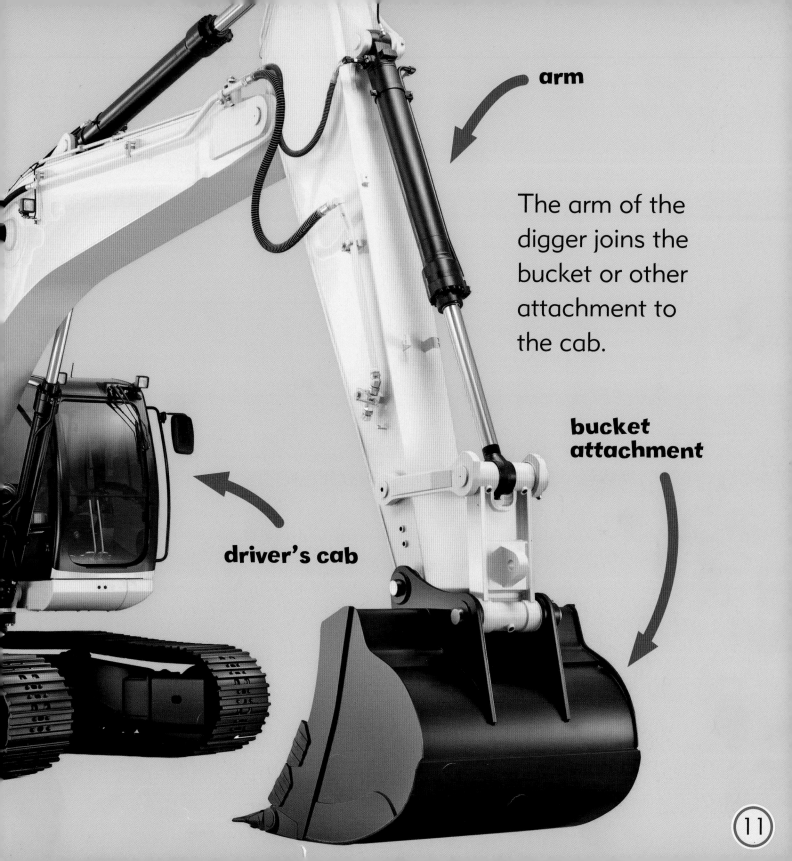

arm

The arm of the digger joins the bucket or other attachment to the cab.

bucket attachment

driver's cab

Buckets

The bucket is at the end of the arm. Buckets are made of metal and come in many shapes and sizes. Each one does a different job.

Some buckets are very wide. The driver uses a wide bucket to scrape up earth or stones.

« A wide bucket collects lots of stones in each scoop.

The teeth on a bucket are large, but not sharp. They push through the ground, just like your teeth bite into food.

teeth

13

Rippers

Diggers with rippers can break through almost any ground, even frozen earth. This means that building work can carry on in almost any weather!

A ripper is an attachment used instead of a bucket. When the ripper crashes into a hard surface, it makes the ground crack.

>> Ripper attachments are sometimes called "teeth."

ripper

<< Some rippers look like single spikes, which hit the hard earth over and over again.

Loaders

These hard-working machines are used to clear ground or dig holes. They load earth or gravel into trucks, which take it away.

>> The driver uses a **lever** to move the bucket.

Loaders usually have two arms which lift and move the bucket at the front.

« The bucket scoops up its load.

» This load is being tipped into the trailer of a road train.

Mining Excavators

Mining **excavators** are big diggers with tracks that are used in **mining**. There are several different types of mining excavators.

>> A dragline excavator loading iron ore into a huge dump truck.

This dragline excavator has a bucket which is moved by steel ropes. One of the ropes moves the bucket up and down. Other ropes move it from side to side.

steel ropes

bucket

arm

Demolition

Diggers can be used to knock down houses and small office blocks. This is called demolition. Diggers **demolish** a building safely, bit by bit.

« The digger's driver controls which way the building falls down.

A digger can demolish tall buildings, too. It has a very long arm that can reach up to the top of the building.

⌃ This digger is very tall. Some diggers are even taller than the Statue of Liberty!

Grabbers

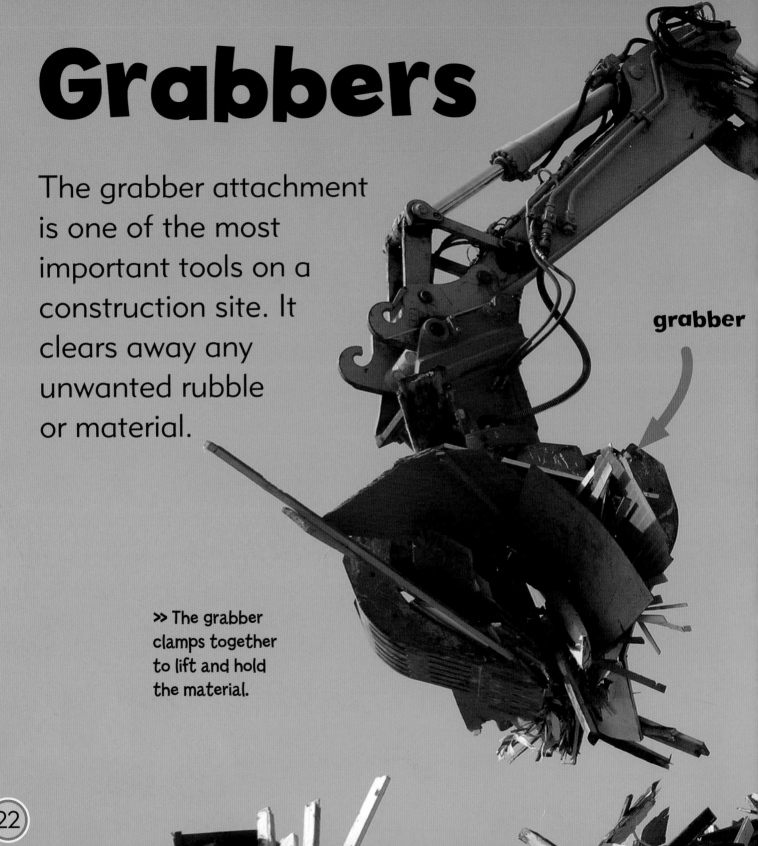

The grabber attachment is one of the most important tools on a construction site. It clears away any unwanted rubble or material.

grabber

>> The grabber clamps together to lift and hold the material.

A grabber is like two buckets that bite together. It is used to lift and carry heavy objects, such as piles of rocks.

>> This digger is lifting heavy logs onto a trailer using a grabber.

Tunnelers

If a road or railway has to cross a river or a hill, the quickest way is often to dig a tunnel under it.

Long, underground tunnels are made by tunnel-boring machines. These rock-eating monsters cut their way through solid rock like long, metal worms.

>> A tunnel-boring machine can carve out 65 feet of finished tunnel a day.

« The huge cutting head of this tunnel borer spins around to cut through rock and earth.

cutting head

Drill Rigs

Some diggers carry a drill **rig**, which is used to dig deep holes in the ground.

⌃ When the truck is moving, the drill is carried flat.

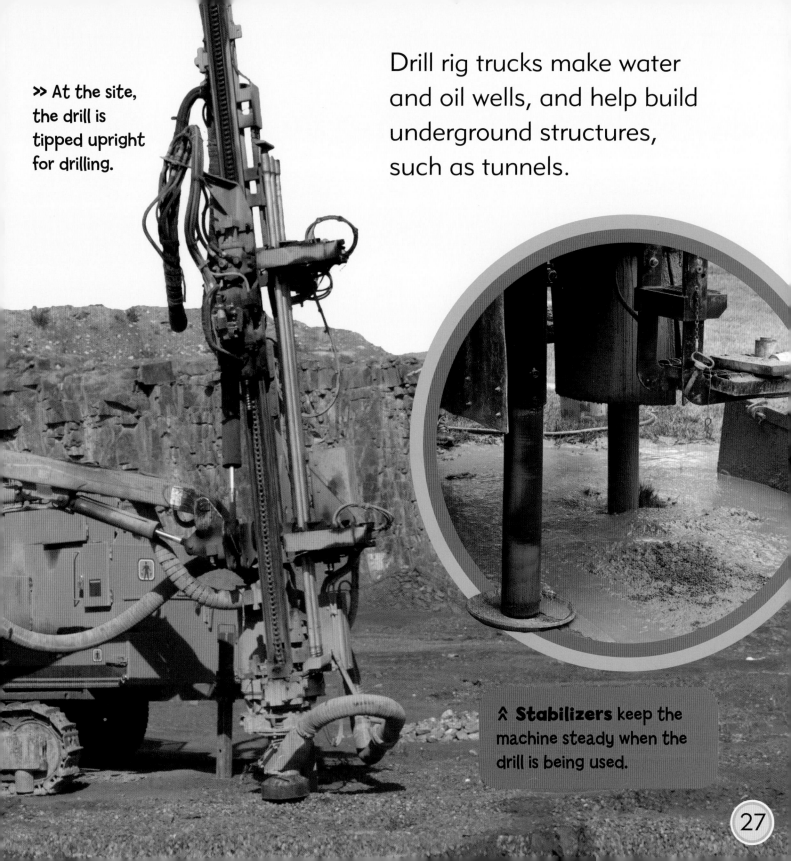

>> At the site, the drill is tipped upright for drilling.

Drill rig trucks make water and oil wells, and help build underground structures, such as tunnels.

⌃ **Stabilizers** keep the machine steady when the drill is being used.

Bulldozers

Bulldozers sound big and strong, and they are! These mighty machines are also called earthmovers.

≪ A ripper at the back breaks up the ground.

>> The blade is used for pushing earth, sand, or heavy objects.

The blade at the front can clear forests or move huge mounds of earth to make the ground flat.

Compactors

Compactors work on **landfill sites**. They are used to crush mounds of garbage, so more can be piled on top.

« The metal spikes on the wheels tear the trash and press it flat.

« The cab has windows on all sides so the driver can see all around.

Compactors have special wheels to do their job. The wheels are huge, heavy, and spiked. As they drive over the trash, they break it up and squash it, so it takes up less space.

« The blade is used to spread waste mounds into flat layers.

Suction Excavators

A suction excavator has a special **hose** to suck up waste. It can be used to remove soil from a hole, or water from a river or swimming pool.

A suction excavator is useful for cleaning **sewage pipes**. It can also clean up river banks without scraping away any of the land.

>> This machine works like a vacuum cleaner to suck up waste into the truck.

>> A suction excavator works hard to empty an area quickly.

Biggest and Smallest

The biggest diggers in the world work in coal mines. One of the biggest diggers is the Rheinbraun 291, measuring 740 feet long. That is the same as 21 school buses!

⌃ This Rheinbraun 291 has huge wheels.

⌄ The Rheinbraun 291 is shown here digging brown-coal in one of the world's deepest mines, in Germany.

There are many mini-diggers. They are used in gardens to clear garden waste, or for small building jobs.

⌄ This is one of the smallest mini-diggers.

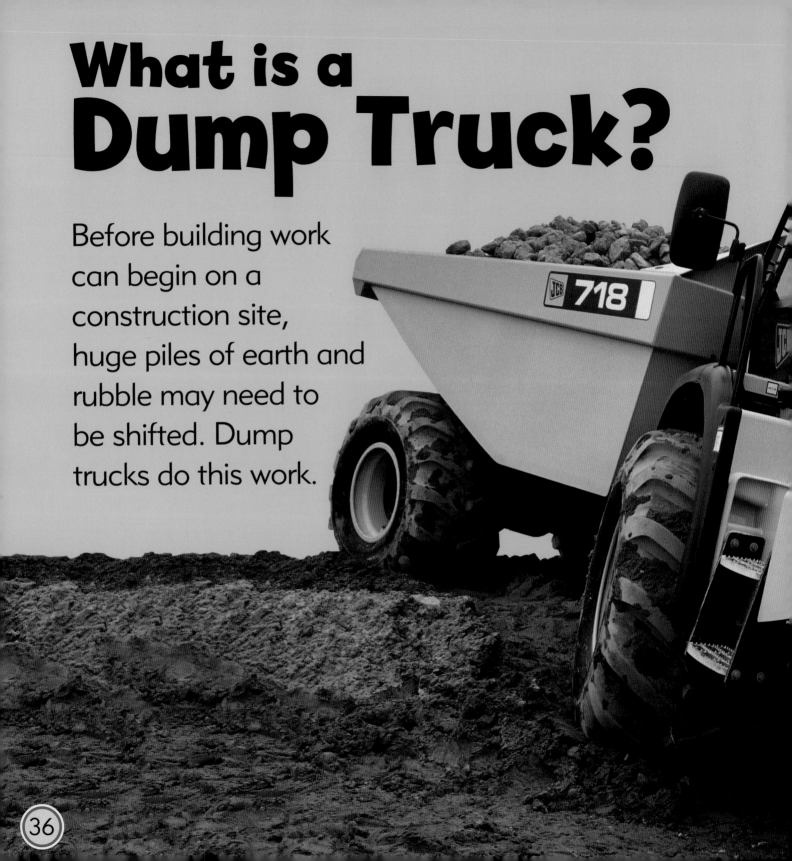

What is a Dump Truck?

Before building work can begin on a construction site, huge piles of earth and rubble may need to be shifted. Dump trucks do this work.

Big trucks also deliver sand, gravel, bricks, and other building materials to the construction site.

⌃ A dump truck tips up at the back to empty its load onto the ground.

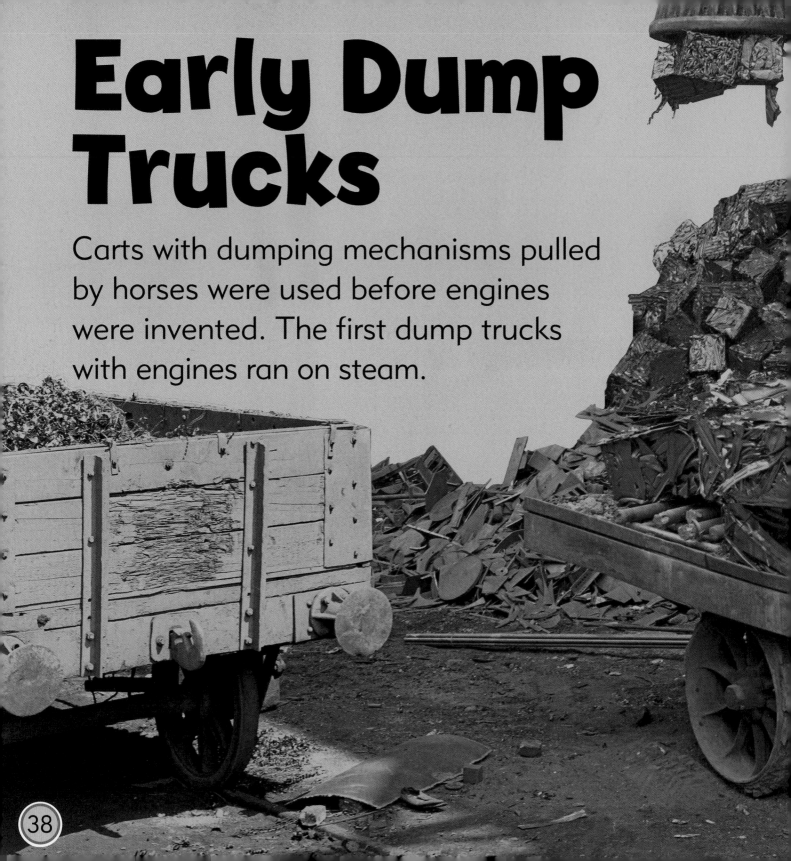

Early Dump Trucks

Carts with dumping mechanisms pulled by horses were used before engines were invented. The first dump trucks with engines ran on steam.

This steam wagon is being loaded with scrap metal at a steel factory in Sheffield, UK.

Parts of a Dump Truck

Most dump trucks have beds that can be raised to dump materials wherever they are needed.

Cab

Engine

Step

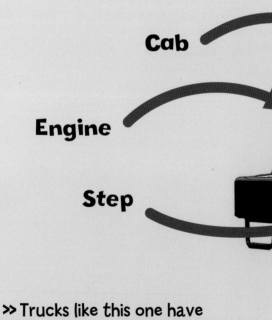

>> Trucks like this one have big tires so that they can move easily on rough ground.

Tires

The driver controls the bed
from the driver's cab.

>> The driver uses a step
to reach the cab of a
dump truck.

Bed

Arm

Tipping Trucks

The bed of a tipping dump truck tips up so that the load slides off where it is needed.

>> The driver controls when to lift the bed of the truck and tip the load out.

⌃ Some trucks tip sideways.

Tipping dump trucks clear away garbage, or transport loads on building sites. They are also used to move coal.

∧ Some trucks have two tipping beds, so they can move even bigger loads.

Concrete Mixers

A concrete mixer has a huge drum filled with cement, sand, gravel, and water.

⌃ Water is stored in a tank behind the cab.

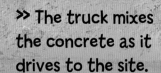

>> The truck mixes the concrete as it drives to the site.

As the drum slowly turns, it mixes everything together to make concrete. Concrete is used to make buildings, sidewalks, and swimming pools.

⌃ A **chute** is used to pour the concrete.

Robot Trucks

Giant, driverless robot trucks have been programmed to work in huge mines. Each truck is as tall as a two-story building.

>> The trucks are controlled using a computer in space.

The trucks work in mines, but are controlled by people in offices over 900 miles away!

˅ The trucks use sensors to avoid crashing into each other.

Snow Plows

These trucks save lives by clearing dangerous ice and snow from roads.

>> Some snow plows carry salt, called grit, to spread on icy roads to melt the ice.

⌃ Sometimes snow chains are used to give extra grip.

Snow plows are used in countries that have a lot of deep snow each year. They help to clear the roads so cars and buses can run normally.

⌃ Snow plows push the snow aside.

Combine Harvesters

A combine harvester is used on farms to gather crops, such as wheat or corn.

⌄ Inside the drum, the grain is separated from the stalks.

⌃ The spinning blades in the front cut the crops.

A combine harvester and a truck work together to collect the grain. The combine cuts the crop, separates the grain from the stalks, and pours the grain into the truck.

⌃ The grain pours out of a long chute.

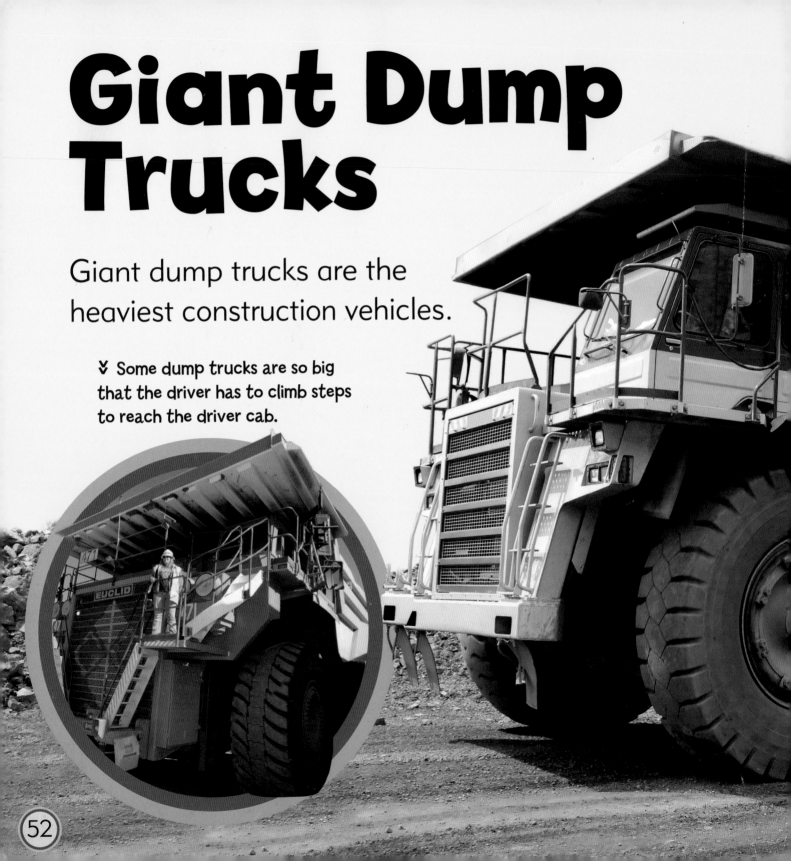

Giant Dump Trucks

Giant dump trucks are the heaviest construction vehicles.

⌄ Some dump trucks are so big that the driver has to climb steps to reach the driver cab.

Huge dump trucks often work in mines and quarries, carrying rock. The rock often contains valuable metals, such as copper.

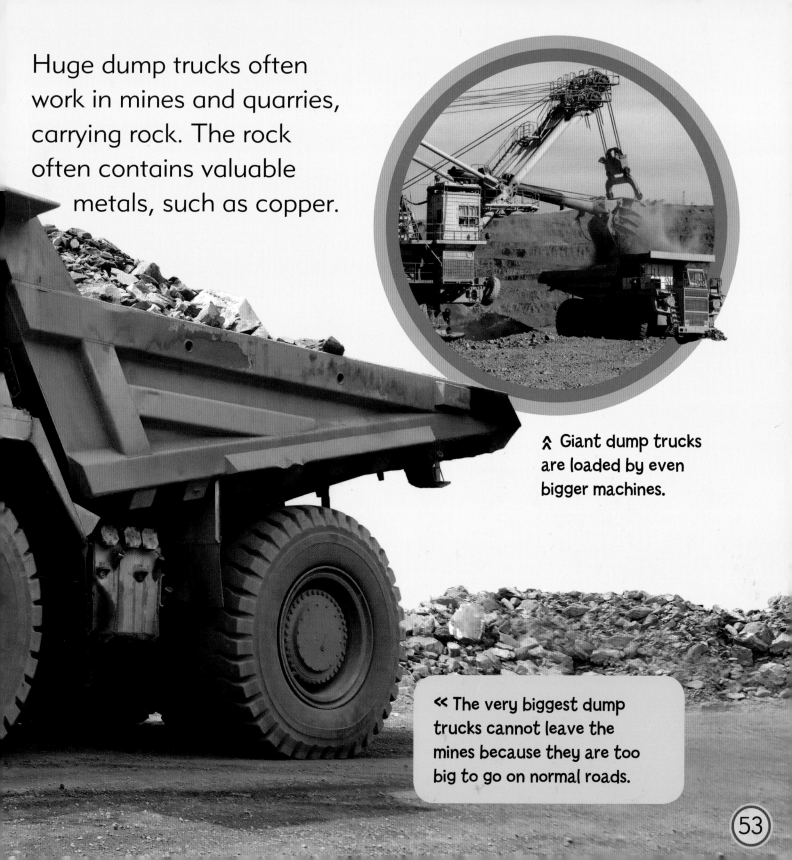

⌃ Giant dump trucks are loaded by even bigger machines.

≪ The very biggest dump trucks cannot leave the mines because they are too big to go on normal roads.

Road Trains

A road train is a truck that pulls lots of trailers joined together. The trailers carry different materials, such as coal, salt, and fuel.

« This road train is carrying salt, which it will tip out where needed.

≪ Road trains travel along the highways.

A record-breaking road train was 112 trailers long with a total length of 4,836 ft 11 in!

Biggest and Smallest

Dump trucks really are the heavyweights of the truck world. But because they are used for a variety of jobs, they come in many different sizes.

75710

<< The Piaggio Ape dump truck is only 10.5 feet long and 5.5 feet high.

>> The world's biggest tire is more than 14 feet tall.

⌃ The world's biggest truck ever is a Belaz 75710 dump truck that is 65 feet long and 26 feet high.

Other Types of Truck

Trucks come in all shapes and sizes. They are used to carry heavy cargo and equipment to where they are needed.

⌃ Flatbed trucks are used to carry large items over long distances.

>> Fire engines carry equipment such as water, hoses, and ladders.

❯ This fast little forklift truck is used to pick up and move bulky loads over short distances.

59

Glossary

attachment A tool on the end of a digger's arm. The tool is usually a bucket.

bucket A large container on the end of a digger's arm. It is used to scoop up earth and stones.

cab The place where the driver sits.

chute A sloping pipe that things can slide down.

construction Another word for building.

demolish To knock down a building.

engine Part of a truck that gives it the power to move.

excavator A digger which removes something from an area.

hose A long pipe or tube.

landfill site A place where garbage is dumped and buried.

lever What the driver pulls to lift or move the digger's arm.

load A big, heavy thing that needs to be carried.

mining Taking coal or valuable materials out of the ground.

quarries Places where stone is blasted or cut from the rocks.

rig Equipment or machinery used for a particular job.

rubble Broken chunks of old stone, brick, or concrete.

sewage pipes Pipes that takes waste away from people's homes and offices.

stabilizers Metal "legs" that help keep a machine upright and keep it from falling over.

trucks Big road or construction vehicles used for moving heavy loads.

Index

A

arms 10, 11, 17, 19, 41

B

beds 41, 42, 43
Belaz 75710 dump truck 57
biggest and smallest diggers 34–35
biggest and smallest dump trucks 56–57
blades 29, 31, 50
bucket-wheel excavators 18
buckets 7, 10, 11, 12–13, 17, 19
bulldozers 28–29

C

cabs 10, 11, 31, 40
chutes 45, 51
combine harvesters 50–51
compactors 30–31
computers 47

concrete mixers 44–45
cutting heads 25

D

Darby Steam-Digger 8
demolition 20–21
diggers 6–35
dragline excavators 19
drill rigs 26–27
drivers 10, 16, 20, 41
drums 44, 45, 50
dump trucks 36–57

E

early diggers 8–9
early dump trucks 38–39
engines 5, 10, 38, 40

F

fire engines 59
flatbed trucks 58
forklift trucks 59

G

giant dump trucks 52–53
grabbers 22–23

H

hoses 32

L

levers 16
loaders 16–17

M

mini-diggers 35
mining excavators 18–19

P

parts of a digger 10–11
parts of a dump truck 40–41
Piaggio Ape 56

R

Rheinbraun 34–35
rippers 14–15, 28
road trains 17, 54–55
robot trucks 46–47

S

sensors 46
sewage pipes 32
snow chains 48
snow plows 48–49

spikes 15, 30, 31
stabilizers 27
steam wagons 38–39
steel ropes 19
steps 40, 52

T

teeth 7, 10, 13, 14
tipping trucks 42–43
tires 40, 57
tracks 6, 10
trailers 54
tunnel-boring machines 24–25

W

wheels 5, 30, 31

Picture credits

(t=top, b=bottom, l=left, r=right, c=center, fc=front cover, bc=back cover)